What is Anthroposophy?

By the same author:

The Case of Valentin Tomberg
The Cycle of the Seasons and the Seven Liberal Arts
The Cycle of the Year as a Path of Initiation
The East in the Light of the West
*The Encounter with Evil and its Overcoming through Spiritual
    Science*
Eternal Individuality, Towards a Karmic Biography of Novalis
The Heavenly Sophia and the Living Being Anthroposophia
May Human Beings Hear It!
The Mystery of John the Baptist and John the Evangelist
The Occult Significance of Forgiveness
Prophecy of the Russian Epic
Rudolf Steiner and the Founding of the New Mysteries
*Rudolf Steiner's Research into Karma and the Mission of the
    Anthroposophical Society*
*The Spiritual Origins of Eastern Europe and the Future Mysteries of
    the Holy Grail*
The Twelve Holy Nights and the Spiritual Hierarchies
Valentin Tomberg and Anthroposophy

What is Anthroposophy?

SERGEI O. PROKOFIEFF

TEMPLE LODGE

Translated from German by Simon Blaxland de Lange

Temple Lodge Publishing
Hillside House, The Square
Forest Row, RH18 5ES

www.templelodge.com

First English edition 2006

Originally published in German under the title *Was ist Anthroposophie?* by Verlag
am Goetheanum, Dornach, in 2004

A catalogue record for this book is available from the British Library

ISBN-10: 1 902636 78 3
ISBN-13: 978 1 902636 78 8

Cover by Andrew Morgan
Typeset by DP Photosetting, Aylesbury, Bucks.
Printed and bound by Cromwell Press Limited, Trowbridge, Wilts.

Contents

Preface

This volume represents the substance of a lecture that I gave at the Annual General Meeting of the Anthroposophical Society in Great Britain on 3 May 2002 in Lampeter, the oldest university in Wales.

In the history of the anthroposophical movement, several authors have made the attempt to describe the nature of anthroposophy and, hence, to give an answer to the question posed. Although giving such an answer might seem a perfectly straightforward task, it is actually not at all simple; for anthroposophy can be characterized from such a variety of aspects that ultimately an attempt of this kind says more about the author himself than about the ostensible subject. And that is justified. For as soon as we comprehend anthroposophy as something living, we are concerned not merely with defining it intellectually but, rather, with developing a real relationship to it such as can only be established by one being to another and must, therefore, necessarily have an individual character.

I should like to make special reference here to some other attempts of this nature (in the German language).

First, the excellent lecture by Carl Unger on 'What is anthroposophy?', which depicts it essentially as a science of the higher ego and takes particular account of its path of schooling. Another is the booklet by Otto Fränkl-Lundborg, in which the author uses a descriptive method to characterize the breadth and manifoldness of the realms where anthroposophy has brought an impulse of renewal. Through its systematic presentation, this approach gives a good overview of its most important orientations. Recently, a third publication in this series from Verlag am Goetheanum has appeared. Karen Swassjan's presentation is one that views anthroposophy in the light of Rudolf Steiner's early work.

A further attempt to grasp the nature of anthroposophy is now being added to this series of publications. Likewise on this occasion, the content will probably reveal more about the author and his relationship to anthroposophy than about it itself, for its nature is basically beyond description and consequently evades any purely intellectual definition. Moreover, one's inner meeting with it is one of the most intimate of soul experiences and cannot, therefore, be presented in a publicly open way.

The essential difference of what follows from the three essays that have been mentioned is that the latter are aimed mainly at those who are not already familiar with anthroposophy. The present essay, in contrast, presupposes an acquaintance with its basic principles, since it has more to do with the central Christological insights that form the essential core of anthroposophy.

With these remarks the author would also address an invitation to other anthroposophists who are seeking, or have already found, an inner relationship with the being of anthroposophy to make a further contribution to the question 'What is anthroposophy?' out of their own experiences on this path.

Sergei Prokofieff, Dornach, July 2004

1. Anthroposophy and the Riddle of Man

The modern epoch, which mankind entered at the beginning of the fifteenth century, is marked pre-eminently by a consistent loss of a true knowledge of the nature of man. This loss with regard to human nature has been accompanied by great successes on the part of science in investigating the natural world and by the ensuing technologies, which, to an ever-greater extent, shape the modern world. Such a loss nevertheless leads to a growing sense of unhappiness at the deeper levels of the human soul and also to existential questions, without an answer to which an existence worthy of man will be ever less possible on Earth.

As a modern science of the spirit, anthroposophy can contribute today to this new search for the being of man. In his autobiography, Rudolf Steiner has characterized this problem as follows: 'The whole world except man is a riddle, the real universal riddle; and *man himself is its solution*' (GA 28, chapter XXII, *The Course of My Life*). In accordance with these words, the riddle of man must first be solved, a riddle that consists above all in the nature of the ego and the ego-consciousness that is associated with it, in order that the various realms of the world around us may rightly be understood. However, human nature has its foundation not in the physical world of the senses but in the spiritual world, which is where the solution to this question is to be sought.

Thus anthroposophy in the first instance represents a modern scientific method, which signifies a continuation and expansion of natural science into the regions of the spiritual world where the true being of man has its origin. With the strict care and precision of a scientist, Rudolf Steiner described—on the basis of his spiritual research—the most diverse supersensible domains in his work, availing himself of the same methods that he had established and employed in his early philosophical writings. The manifold practical implementations of the results of his research substantiate the scientific quality and thoroughness of anthroposophy.

| The early philosophical work. Cognitive foundations of anthroposophy. | Anthroposophy as a modern science of the spirit. | Practical implementation of its results in the various domains of life. |

2. The Anthroposophical Path of Knowledge

I n his fundamental work *The Philosophy of Freedom*, Rudolf Steiner described the process of scientific knowledge as consisting of two aspects: of percepts coming outwardly through the senses, and concepts arising from within the human soul. Only their uniting on the part of the human ego through the living activity of thinking creates a full reality. In this unifying activity of the ego, however, world processes are not merely passively mirrored but man himself enters actively and creatively into world evolution.

If one looks carefully at the former realm, one may conclude that percepts are not by any means made up only of the impressions of the sense-world. On the contrary, they also include all inner percepts that can be engendered in the course of self-observation: memories, emotions, sympathies and antipathies.

The other aspect of the cognitive process, concepts, which our thinking derives from the all-encompassing sphere of ideas with the help of the faculty of intuition, is characterized by the highest level of awareness attainable to man. For only in thinking is earthly man fully conscious. Already in his feelings he has a less heightened state of awareness, which can be compared with dreams. In the sphere of the will, on the other hand, man is wholly asleep. Thus in general the activity that follows our resolve to take hold of an object with our hand and then extends into the outer movement of our muscles does not enter our consciousness.

One of the first fruits of self-observation is the realization that the clarity and precision of thinking are at the same time associated with its shadowlike aspect. One needs only to gaze upon a beautiful mountain landscape, then close one's eyes and compare the actual sight with one's thoughts about it. However, this shadowlike aspect does not derive from our thinking itself but emerges only with our incarnation through union with the physical body or, to be more precise, with the brain. The relationship that pertains here is also confirmed through the fact that where the brain is impaired conscious thinking is no longer possible. Consequently, man's ordinary thinking is orientated mainly around the impressions of the sense organs. But precisely because of this close connection with the physical body and its senses, *this* thinking can never apprehend the spiritual world. The reason for this lies in the fact that nothing that is in whatever way connected with the physical world of the senses is able to penetrate into the sphere of the supersensible.

Something else that one can learn just as surely

through self-observation and which one finds fully established in *The Philosophy of Freedom* is that thinking is in itself a *supersensible* activity taking place within man, which is directly connected with the inner experience of the human ego. The question that arises here is: Why is it that in the course of human life this essentially supersensible activity is associated with the physical brain? Or, in Rudolf Steiner's formulation of the question: 'If the human organization has no part in the *essential nature* of thinking, what is the significance of this organization within the whole nature of man?' (*The Philosophy of Freedom*, chapter 9,[1] the italics are Rudolf Steiner's). In *The Philosophy of Freedom* Rudolf Steiner answers this question as follows: 'Now, what happens in this organization through the thinking has indeed nothing to do with the essence of thinking, but it has a great deal to do with the arising of ego-consciousness out of this thinking. Thinking, in its own essential nature, certainly contains the real I or ego, but it does not contain ego-consciousness'.

Rudolf Steiner goes on to say that the nature of the ego can only be grasped within the thinking, whereas 'ego-consciousness' arises through the involvement of the bodily organization. Ego-consciousness is dependent upon the framework of the body only for the moment of its arising; immediately afterwards it can exist independently of it. 'Once arisen, it is taken up into thinking and shares henceforth in thinking's spiritual being'.

To illustrate the significance of the bodily organization for the arising of 'ego-consciousness', Rudolf Steiner often used the picture of a mirror. Just as a person uses a mirror in order to discover the colour of his eyes or the shape of his nose without identifying himself with the mirror, so does man's ego need the 'mirror' of the human brain and in a fuller sense the whole body with the nervous system that permeates it in order to become conscious of itself. Among the most important conditions of this mirroring process is the fact that the mirror itself is a *dead* object and consequently reproduces in the most exact way only what is in front of it and adds nothing from out of itself.

The same thing happens with the mirror-function of the human brain. That is why it bears the greatest concentration of death forces in the human body. Even in academic physiology it is known today that all forms of man's conscious activity are accompanied by a death-process of nerves in his organism, of which feeling tired in the evening is a consequence. During sleep these dead nerve cells are for the most part renewed. It is also known from physiology that after a person's clinical death the first signs of decay occur in the brain already in the first five minutes, because there is no blood flowing through it and it is therefore no longer nourished by life-forces from the rest of the organism, whereas in the other parts of the body the life-processes are able to continue for several weeks after death.

Only because of this great concentration of death-forces is the brain best suited to take on the role of a mirror for the arising of ego-consciousness. For 'in order to make ego-consciousness our own during life on Earth, our physical body, with its brain organization, has to be a reflecting apparatus' (GA 131, 11 October 1911, *From Jesus to Christ*).

It follows from what has been said that the death-forces that we bear within our bodily organization are utterly necessary for the arising of ego-consciousness on the Earth. With this it is also possible to answer the question why we have to incarnate in a physical body: it is necessary in order to arrive at an individual ego-consciousness which alone goes to make our human nature what it is.

From this original link between ego-consciousness and physical brain there does, however, arise the danger that man gradually gets used to thinking only with his brain, that is, that he regards the dead, shadowlike character of his thoughts as being their only possible manifestation. In this case man develops a way of being conscious on the Earth which is immediately extinguished on entering the spiritual world. For the spiritual world cannot be consciously experienced by means of a thinking that remains bound to the physical body and, hence, is able to understand only what is perceived through the senses.

And yet man unequivocally needs his thinking in the spiritual world if he is to be able to be there in full consciousness. This means, therefore, that thinking must be separated from the bodily organization in order to be able to enter the spiritual world as sense-free thinking. Rudolf Steiner indicates the path to this goal in his *Philosophy of Freedom*. There he speaks of the so-called 'exceptional state' where, through the strengthening of his own thinking—a process in which he himself is active—a person makes this thinking the object of his perception and thereby associates the engendering of thinking and its observation within the same thinking-process in a unity. The difference between *this* association and all others, where the object under observation lies outside the observer, is that here both elements, what is thought and what is perceived, are of the same substance in that they both consist of the nature of thinking.

In this sense 'observation of the thinking itself is a kind of exceptional state' (p. 24), where thinking is self-supporting and does not rely on the physical organization of the brain and, hence, attains a pure, sense-free activity. Only with this kind of thinking, which springs from the exceptional condition described, can man enter the spiritual world. Moreover, in the spiritual world itself this thinking becomes a new organ of perception for spiritual processes and beings, which at this stage of supersensible life appear in the form of *Imaginations* in man's field of consciousness.

Three stages of higher knowledge are spoken of in anthroposophy. Rudolf Steiner calls them Imagination, Inspiration and Intuition. At the stage of Imagination one perceives in picture form only the outward manifestations of spiritual beings. At the stage of Inspiration one experiences their deeds and interrelationships. And only at the third and highest stage, that of Intuition, does one unite oneself with their inner world through the intrinsic union of one being with another, without losing one's own ego (see GA 12, *The Stages of Higher Knowledge*).

If one would advance on the path that has been described from Imagination to Inspiration, it is necessary to make one's feeling as sense-free at this second stage as thinking was at the first, so that—thus freed from all influences of the body—it can become a new organ of perception for Inspirations.[2] This happens through the meditative exercises given by Rudolf Steiner in many of his writings and lectures, above all in his book *Knowledge of the Higher Worlds, How is it Achieved?* (GA 10). This feeling that has become independent from the body is thereby constantly imbued with the thinking that has previously been made independent of it. For only through being thus imbued can the dreamy feeling quality be brought to full consciousness in ordinary life and, hence, be transformed into an organ of higher knowledge.

A similar process occurs at the third stage, that of Intuition, though now with man's will. This is raised by body-free thinking into full human consciousness and is transformed through the corresponding meditative exercises into a still higher cognitive organ, which can accordingly experience Intuitions. Here, at the level of Intuition, a human being can make contact with the true nature of his own ego and also spiritual beings through inwardly merging with them. Thus knowledge at this highest stage has the character of spiritual communion.

That this anthroposophical path of schooling is a direct continuation of *The Philosophy of Freedom* is attested by the following words of Rudolf Steiner: 'If one is seeking a cosmic philosophy to match this philosophy of freedom, it is necessary to expand what has previously been done with reference to a limited field by cultivating the different stages of knowledge: object-based perception, Imagination, Inspiration and Intuition' (GA 78, 3 September 1921, *The Fruits of Anthroposophy*). Thus it befits the anthroposophical viewpoint that human thinking ascends through the meditations and other spiritual exercises given by Rudolf

Steiner to higher stages of knowledge, in order to enter in full consciousness into the supersensible world where alone the riddle of man can be solved.

3. Ego-Consciousness and the Mystery of Golgotha

There is a fundamental problem associated with what was said in the previous section. If ego-consciousness can arise only on the foundation of the mirroring of the ego through the bodily organization and man generally only knows this ego-consciousness that depends upon the body, what happens with it when a human being must leave his physical body at death? The answer is clear: in this case he to a large extent loses his ego-consciousness. Only in so far as a person himself recalls in his existence after death the actual moment of death, that is, the moment of leaving his physical body and, hence, also the latter itself, is he able to maintain something of his ego-consciousness in the spiritual world (see GA 168, 24 October 1916, 'The Problem of Destiny', Typescript NSL 185).

The ancient Greeks were fully aware of the tragedy of this: the most radiant consciousness that they developed purely in the body through the unfolding of philosophical thinking could not be taken with them into the life after death, because the body that served as a mirror was lacking there. And if they left their body in the

Mysteries equipped with sense-free thinking and thereby formed conscious perceptions in the spiritual world, this happened only because they remained connected with the body through feeling and will. If, however, a person persevered so far on the path of the Mysteries that he made also his feeling and above all his will body-free, he no longer had any hold upon himself on entering the spiritual world and entered into it like a single drop in the ocean. He was not capable of maintaining his individuality—or, to be more precise, his ego-consciousness—in it. For he was unable to take the forces of death, which man needed for his ego-consciousness on the Earth, with him into the spiritual world. Thus the Greek was after his death only able to dwell in the spiritual world in a diminished state of consciousness and as a result experienced it in a shadowy way.

Among Eastern mystics one therefore finds even today the indication that the ultimate goal of their inner development is the attainment of the great Samadhi (Nirvakalpasamadhi). This is described by, for example, the yogi Ramakrishna (1836–86), who spent nearly a third of his life outside his body in the condition of Samadhi—the condition of a blissful dissolving of the human individuality in the ocean of divine light.

The problem that arises here can be pointedly formulated as follows. How can one continue to be an ego-being once one has left the physical body at death? For on the Earth it is only through being present in his body that man attains a full ego-consciousness, which, however—for as long as a person thinks only with his brain—is associated with the feeling that it will inevitably be lost at death. On the other hand, if one enters the spiritual world and would seek to attain there immortality of the soul (which is always associated with the cessation of bodily thinking), one experiences the constant danger of losing one's individual ego-consciousness, as is the case with Eastern Samadhi. On Earth one lives as a human being endowed with an ego without the possibility of taking one's ego-consciousness into the afterlife, because the death-forces at work in the body cannot be taken into the spiritual world. And in the spiritual world this ego-consciousness cannot be fully developed because the death (or bodily) forces that are needed for it are lacking there.

In sum, this initially insoluble problem can be thus characterized: on Earth the ego exists without immortality, and in the spiritual world it is the other way round—what exists there is immortality of the soul, but without ego-consciousness.

This state of affairs can also be described in another way. For as long as a human individual is dwelling in his physical body, his three soul-members of thinking, feeling and will—whose cohesion within the physical body forms the basis of his ego-consciousness—are held together by this body. Once he has crossed the threshold, thinking, feeling and will separate; and they would wholly lose their connection with one another—corresponding to the dissolving of a drop in the ocean—if they did not find a new cohesiveness now that the physical body has been left. What is this new cohesion?

Rudolf Steiner has spoken in a number of lectures of how, as a significant step in its evolution, Western humanity unconsciously crossed the threshold of the spiritual world already in the nineteenth century (see, for example, GA 233a, 12 January 1924, *Rosicrucianism and Modern Initiation*). The consequence that results from this is that symptoms manifest themselves in our life that are associated with a drifting apart of the three soul-forces, as can be increasingly observed in the various phenomena of illness and decay in modern civilization.

In his book *Knowledge of the Higher Worlds* (GA 10) Rudolf Steiner describes how, through a consistently pursued path of knowledge, man's ego can be strengthened to the extent that it is increasingly enabled to be not subject to these symptoms of decay and also to maintain the connection between thinking, feeling and will—and, hence, its ego-consciousness—in the life after death.

If this path of schooling is followed sufficiently far, it leads the person following it to an encounter with the

Greater Guardian of the Threshold and, hence, with the Christ Himself (see GA 13, *Occult Science*).

And now the question posed earlier can be answered. The new source of cohesion for the diverging soul-forces can be found on the path that leads man from his ordinary, earthly ego to his higher ego and finally to an encounter with the World Ego of the Christ. Or to put it another way: already here on Earth a person needs to find at least an initial relationship to the Ego of Christ and, hence, also to His deed in the Mystery of Golgotha, so that he can maintain his ego-consciousness beyond the threshold.

For only through this deed of Christ was the decisive question about the continuing existence of the human personality after death answered on a world-historical plane once and for the entire future of human evolution. This happened not in some sort of theoretical way but as the cosmically earthly fact of the *Resurrection* of Christ Jesus.

In many instances in his lectures and writings, Rudolf Steiner has indicated that, in contrast to all other world religions, the nature of Christianity consists in that it was not a new revelation of wisdom that came into the world through it but, rather, a unique spiritually physical *deed* that was accomplished which has given the whole of earthly evolution its significance. Rudolf Steiner describes the nature of this deed as the fashioning of the 'imperishable body' or 'phantom' through Christ's Resurrection. 'For the important thing [about Christianity] is not what Christ Jesus taught but what He gave to humanity. His Resurrection is the birth-process of a new member of man's being: an imperishable body' (GA 131, 11 October 1911, *From Jesus to Christ*). Likewise the Apostle Paul refers to this distinctive trait of Christianity in the following words: 'If Christ has not been raised, your faith is futile' (I Corinthians 15:17).

In this sense one can also understand why Rudolf Steiner characterizes Christianity as something that indeed begins as a religion but as regards its deeper nature is more than any religion: 'Christianity was a religion in its origins but it is greater than all religion.' It is 'even greater than the religious principle itself' (GA 102, 24 March 1908, *The Influence of Spiritual Beings Upon Man*). For the word religion means 'reconnection', which only applies to the religions of wisdom, since these try through new revelations of wisdom to link humanity again to its primal source in the spiritual world. They are therefore all backwards looking. They want to lead human beings back into a primal Paradise. In Christianity, on the other hand, one is not principally concerned with wisdom but with a single deed of the Christ in the Mystery of Golgotha and its consequences for the entirety of human and earthly evolution. Thus Christianity—when rightly understood—is something that is wholly oriented towards the future and can, therefore, only be apocalyptic in the present.

In what, however, does this deed of Christ consist? From the sources of his spiritual research Rudolf Steiner characterizes this in the central Christological lecture-cycle *From Jesus to Christ*. Here he describes how man's ego, consciousness of which has from the outset been associated with the mirroring function of the physical body, would through the gradual disintegration of the latter in the course of time have inexorably fallen into oblivion. For the consequence of the so-called Fall and the associated intervention of Luciferic and Ahrimanic forces into human evolution was that the physical body became ever harder and increasingly became subject to death. The ancient Greek experienced this process in the following way: 'And when he saw the form of the physical body falling into decadence, he shuddered at the thought that his ego would grow dark and dim—this ego which is enabled to evolve only through being reflected by the form of the physical body.' Hence there existed 'the danger for the whole evolution of humanity . . . that ego-consciousness—the specific achievement of Earth evolution—would be lost' (GA 131, 11 October 1911). And in the same lecture he goes on to describe how without the maintaining of this ego-consciousness man's ego itself would in time be destroyed. Thus Rudolf Steiner could say that we must 'come to regard the Mystery of Golgotha as a reality that took place and had to take place in the evolution of the Earth; for it signifies literally *the rescuing of the human ego*'.

By this means man's ego, the central achievement of earthly evolution, was rescued not only for the period of life in the physical body but above all also for the after-life and, indeed, for life in the spiritual world altogether. In this way an eternal character was given to the ego itself—but on one condition, that already here on Earth it finds a conscious relationship to the Mystery of Golgotha, that is, to the Resurrection body or phantom of Christ. For only through this might man be enabled to take a form of the body into the life after death which continues to exist to its full extent in the spiritual world and thereby serves man as a 'mirror' for the maintaining of his ego-consciousness in the supersensible domain.

In pre-Christian times, from the time that ego-consciousness had been achieved through the body, one was able to take only as much of it into the life after death as one could after one's death, or to be more precise at the moment of death, remember of the physical form that had been left behind. This memory did, however, fade for the soul soon after death, and the sense of ego-consciousness became correspondingly more hazy, with the result that shortly afterwards one could experience the spiritual world in no more than a shadowy way. The famous words of Achilles in Homer's *Odyssey*—'better to be a beggar in the upper world than a king in the realm of the shades'—refer to this state of affairs. Moreover, with the intensifying degeneracy of the physical body on the Earth ego-consciousness becomes ever weaker, with the result that the human ego would in time ultimately forfeit its immortality as an individual being.

Thus the problem of the immortality of the ego after death could only be solved through an earthly body being created which is able to exist both in the earthly and also in the supersensible domains, thus ensuring the maintaining of human ego-consciousness equally on Earth and in the spiritual world.

This body, which is both supersensible and physical, was fashioned by the Christ through His Resurrection. It is the unshakeable foundation for the rescuing of the individual human ego for the entire future of earthly evolution. Thus Rudolf Steiner could say regarding man's future relationship to the Christ: ' "Christ gives me my humanity"—that will be the fundamental feeling which will well up in the soul and pervade it' (GA 26, 9 November 1924, *Anthroposophical Leading Thoughts*).

The nature of the human ego and the further development of ego-consciousness have from the outset a central significance for anthroposophy, which is, therefore, inseparably associated with the Mystery of Golgotha and its consequences for the evolution of humanity. For in the view of anthroposophy the ultimate solution of the riddle of man lies in the mystery of the human ego, which without the Mystery of Golgotha is able neither to exist nor be perceived. Hence the Being of Christ and His unique deed on the Hill of Golgotha stand at the centre of what it has to impart, as Rudolf Steiner indicates in the following words: 'That is why the anthroposophical world-conception sees the Christ Being as a focal point in the whole panorama of reincarnation, the being of man, study of the cosmos and so forth. And whoever studies this anthroposophical world-conception in its true sense will say to himself: I can contemplate all that, but I can comprehend it only when the whole picture focuses upon the great central point, the Christ' (GA 112, 30 June 1909, *The Gospel of St John and its Relation to the Other Gospels*).

Thus anthroposophy is the central stream of esoteric Christianity for our time. It is Christian not only because Rudolf Steiner gave many lectures on Christian themes and incredibly much to elucidate the Mystery of Golgotha, the Gospels and the Being of Christ in its earthly and cosmic aspects, but also because the research and cognitive method of anthroposophy is itself Christian, whether it be concerned with Christian themes or with those which would appear to be far removed from it.

For the source of anthroposophy lies in the nature of the Resurrection itself. Thus the inner Resurrection process within man already begins with thinking livingly and intensively about the substance of spiritual science. Then with the extension of this process to the realm of feeling and finally to that of the will (which is possible only after embarking upon the path of schooling), there begins the incorporation of the phantom into the being of man, leading to an actual encounter with the Christ in the Resurrection sphere.

All practical implementations of anthroposophy (the so-called daughter movements) have also arisen out of this source of knowledge and creativity. Whether it be a Waldorf school or an anthroposophical bank, anthroposophical medicine or curative education, the new art of eurythmy and creative speech or the renewal of the plastic arts, impulses in the various fields of science or the social life of mankind (threefolding of the social organism)—wherever the many areas of practical life are renewed and transformed out of an understanding of anthroposophy, one is in truth dealing with the concrete application of Resurrection forces.

Anthroposophy is as regards its method and, hence, also in all the practical results that it has engendered, a *Resurrection science*. It is a scientific path, which leads modern man to a knowledge of and an involvement with the Resurrection.

4. Rudolf Steiner's Path of Development

Of a unique significance in this respect is the spiritual development of Rudolf Steiner himself, who through his life anticipated the new faculties which other people will attain only in the distant future. By this means he has manifested to humanity the entire perspective and significance of the Christ consciousness, which he succeeded in achieving.

This path of development, which culminated in a conscious relationship with the forces of the Resurrection body that form the spiritual point of departure for anthroposophy, can be understood only on the basis of what Rudolf Steiner had already presented in his *Philosophy of Freedom*. In this book it is described how through the attainment of intuitive thinking a path can be taken into the spiritual world which at its end leads to an experiencing of the Resurrection body as a source of immortality for human ego-consciousness. For the book's central problem, that of freedom, is inseparable from the experiencing of the immortality of man's being, that is to say, his ego. 'But one will not be conscious of freedom if one is not conscious of the immortal essence of man ... To the extent that mortal man raises the immortal element within himself ever more and more to the nature of consciousness will he also be conscious of his freedom' (lecture of 1 May 1918, not translated). In order to make this 'immortal man' within oneself fully conscious, one must first fathom the nature of ego-consciousness to its very foundations. This is possible only if one encounters the death-forces that are at work there.[3]

For without experiencing this, 'the communication of human consciousness with itself' cannot be brought to its ultimate end. That is why this path led Rudolf Steiner to the realm where the death-forces giving rise to ego-consciousness originated. With his spirit he had to traverse this realm, which is inhabited by death-bringing ahrimanic beings in the spiritual world directly bordering on the earthly world (see GA 28, chapter 26, *Autobiography*).

This conscious engagement with death-forces signified for Rudolf Steiner a probation of life and death dimensions. It is altogether the greatest crisis that one can experience on the path of modern initiation. In a personally existential way the question that arose before Rudolf Steiner was: How can one exist in the realm of death without dying in one's consciousness, that is, as an ego-being? The practical answer to this question, which brought with it the only valid solution to this problem, was the establishing of a conscious relationship to the

Mystery of Golgotha as the innermost core of Christianity. 'In this time of testing I succeeded in progressing further only when in spiritual vision I brought before my mind the evolution of Christianity . . . After the time of testing had subjected me to stern battles of the soul, I had to submerge myself in Christianity and, indeed, in the world in which it is spoken of by the spirit' (GA 28, chapter 26, *Autobiography*).

This spiritual path, which brought Rudolf Steiner to the verge of death, as happened in the Mysteries of all ages, then culminated in his breakthrough to the essential nature of the Mystery of Golgotha, which he describes in his autobiography as follows: 'My soul development rested upon the fact that I had stood in spirit before the Mystery of Golgotha in most inward, most earnest solemnity of knowledge'.

It is significant that Rudolf Steiner does not mention the name of Christ here but refers directly to the Mystery of Golgotha, to this central deed of Christ whereby the Resurrection body originated. In this way he is referring to the most essential aspect of this experience: its connection with the forces of the Resurrection body. Rudolf Steiner described this experience from a purely objective aspect at the end of the chapter on initiation in his book *Occult Science* (GA 13) as an encounter with the Christ at the highest stage of Intuition which, he says, alone leads to a true knowledge of the Mystery of

Golgotha and, hence, the Resurrection body. For to understand Christ's Golgotha deed in Intuition means at the same time to unite oneself existentially with its essence, which signifies a spiritual communion with the Resurrection body.[4]

Only this intrinsic union with the forces of the Resurrection body can make the riddle of the exceptional spiritual capacities of the founder of anthroposophy comprehensible. For only a connection with these forces enables a human being fully to maintain his ego-consciousness at all stages and in all spheres of the spiritual world (extending to the very highest). And only a person who can consciously perceive, and can describe and portray in clear concepts, the beings and phenomena of the spiritual world with the same thoroughness and precision as a modern scientist achieves with regard to the processes of nature can be called a true spirit-researcher.

Thus one can say that only through this initiation-experience did the founding of anthroposophy become at all possible. Hence one can only answer the question 'What is anthroposophy?' if one includes in one's answer to this question the developmental path of Rudolf Steiner, which led to its coming into being. For the greatest open secret of anthroposophy is the mystery of its founder.

5. The Being of the Christ and the Mystery of Man

The relationship described above of the modern Christian initiate to the Resurrection body has a further consequence for the initiate himself. In order to understand this, one must take into account the fact that in the case of every human being there is a particular relationship of his human ego to the form of the physical body that belongs to it at any one time. So as to come to self-consciousness, every human ego forms— to an extent while still in the pre-birth state and then also in the first three years of earthly life—its own physical sheath in such a way that this can subsequently serve it as a complete 'mirror-apparatus' for the arising of ego-consciousness. In accordance with the karma deriving from its previous incarnations that is associated with the ego, each human ego builds for itself a bodily vessel that is suited uniquely to it alone.

This unique correspondence between an individual ego and the physical body belonging to it existed also in the case of the incarnation of the Christ. Thus in the course of the three years of His earthly life the World Ego of the Christ transformed the bodily sheath of Jesus

of Nazareth, which had been sacrificed to Him, into a
new body that, after His Resurrection, wholly corre-
sponded to this World Ego in all its members. This had
the consequence that in modern initiation the connection with the Resurrection body is also the path
whereby one may encounter the Christ as the cosmic
archetype of the ego. For this body of Christ reflects
back the forces of its divine Ego and so leads to an
encounter with it. What happens as a result of this
essential encounter comes to expression in the words of
the Foundation Stone Meditation:

> Thine own I
> Unite
> With the World-I
> (GA 260, 25 December 1923, *The Christmas Conference*).

As the divine 'I Am' the Ego of the Christ now unites
with the human ego, so that for it the words of Paul 'Not
I but the Christ in me' (Galatians 2:20) become a fully
lived reality.

Rudolf Steiner often spoke of how for Christian
esotericism the seven 'I Am' sayings from the Gospel of
St John are no ordinary linguistic formulas but are per-
sonal testimonies of the Christ as the God of the human
ego. 'The true unique name of the Christ is "I Am";
whoever does not know this does not understand and
calls Him something different. Such a person knows

nothing whatever about Him. "I Am" is His only name' (GA 266/1, 27 May 1909, not translated). Thus the riddle of the human ego can be solved in a fully valid way only by receiving the Ego of Christ into one's own ego at the stage of Intuition, which means, essentially, in an act of the highest spiritual communion. In this way the primal affinity of man's true ego with the cosmic Word itself becomes apparent to him.[5]

The fundamental law of ego development, namely, karma and reincarnation,[6] also becomes discernible to man in a new way, because this manifests itself to him now out of his own experience in the light of Christ as the Lord of Karma.

Through this, man recognizes the full profundity of the words quoted above, 'Christ gives me my humanity'. For Christ encompasses within Himself the mystery of the human ego and also of the future of mankind as the tenth hierarchy, the hierarchy of freedom and love which will arise from the full development of this ego.

And if a human being traverses the path of *The Philosophy of Freedom* to its end, he learns through implementing its first part to know man's true *freedom* in achieving intuitive thinking; and through implementing its second part he develops—on the foundation of this intuitive thinking—the capacity so to act out of pure *love* for an object that his sole motive for action becomes an 'intuition steeped in love' (GA 4, *The Philosophy of*

Freedom, chapter 9). Through this alone will his deed be free and the human individual himself begins to realize the ideal of the tenth hierarchy, recognizing in Christ the highest archetype of this ideal.

What a human individual achieves here within himself is akin to that which corresponds to his free deeds macrocosmically in the universe, in accordance with the cosmic law that like always aspires towards like. Now the person concerned recognizes that Christ accomplished something in the Mystery of Golgotha through His divine moral intuition similar to what man himself brings about out of his human moral intuition.

From this inner relationship of the free human deed with the cosmic deed of the Christ, who as a God has nevertheless Himself lived as one human being among others on the Earth, there arises in the soul a new knowledge of Christ which Rudolf Steiner describes as follows: 'Yes, indeed, it is possible to attain to the imagination of the hill on which the Cross was raised, that Cross on which there hung a God in a human body, a God who out of His own free will—that is to say, out of love—accomplished the act whereby the Earth and humanity could reach their goal' (GA 131, 14 October 1911, *From Jesus to Christ*). Christ accomplished the sacrifice of Golgotha out of the highest moral intuition, that is, out of the purest freedom and love, in order to share its consequences with every human being.

Only a person who out of himself rises through intuitive thinking to moral intuitions, and, hence, manifests freedom and love in his cognitive and practical activity, is able to unite himself with the essential nature of the Mystery of Golgotha and thereby with the Christ Himself. 'The event of Golgotha is a cosmic deed, and free. Springing from the universal love, it is intelligible only by the love in man' (GA 26, leading thought 143, 4 January 1925, *Anthroposophical Leading Thoughts*).

To summarize one can say: anthroposophy is a path which, on the foundation of Resurrection forces, leads man as an ego-being to his full self-fulfilment as a tenth hierarchy.

The reader who is interested in this essay may find a further development of the themes touched upon here in the forthcoming book (spring 2007):

Sergei O. Prokofieff
Anthroposophy and The Philosophy of Freedom

Contents
Introduction

Notes

1. Quotations from this book are taken, with very minor adaptations, from Michael Wilson's translation, first published in 1964.
2. See further in Carl Unger, *Was ist Anthroposophie?*, Dornach 1996.
3. See further regarding Rudolf Steiner's spiritual path from *The Philosophy of Freedom* to the Christ experience in: S. O. Prokofieff, *May Human Beings Hear It!, The Mystery of the Christmas Conference*, chapter 7, '*The Philosophy of Freedom* and the Christmas Conference'; also especially the second part of the book *Rudolf Steiner und die Meister des esoterischen Christentums* (Rudolf Steiner and the Masters of Esoteric Christianity): in preparation.
4. See further in: S. Prokofieff, *May Human Beings Hear It!, The Mystery of the Christmas Conference*, ch. 9: 'The Foundation Stone Meditation, Karma and Resurrection'.
5. That man's true ego derives from the essential nature of the cosmic Word, see further in: S. O. Prokofieff, *May Human Beings Hear It!, The Mystery of the Christmas Conference*, ch. 4, 'The Foundation Stone Meditation in Eurythmy'.
6. See Rudolf Steiner, *Theosophy* (GA 10), the chapter entitled 'Re-embodiment of the Spirit and Destiny (Reincarnation and Karma)'.

Bibliography

All references in the text are supplied with a GA (*Gesamtausgabe*) number indicating from which volume of Rudolf Steiner's Collected Works a quotation or other reference comes. Unless specifically stated, all italicized words or phrases derive from the author. English titles are given in accordance with the version consulted by the translator, and these appear at the relevant point in the text. Full publication details are listed below.

By Rudolf Steiner:

Anthroposophical Leading Thoughts, Rudolf Steiner Press 1973
Autobiography, Anthroposophic Press 1999
The Christmas Conference, Anthroposophic Press 1990
From Jesus to Christ, Rudolf Steiner Press 1991
Fruits of Anthroposophy, Rudolf Steiner Press 1986
The Gospel of John and its Relation to the Other Gospels, Anthroposophic Press 1982
The Influence of Spiritual Beings Upon Man, Anthroposophic Press 1982
Knowledge of the Higher Worlds, Rudolf Steiner Press 1969
Occult Science, An Outline, Rudolf Steiner Press 1979
The Philosophy of Freedom, Rudolf Steiner Press 1964
Rosicrucianism and Modern Initiation, Rudolf Steiner Press 1982

Stages of Higher Knowledge, Anthroposophic Press 1967
Theosophy, Rudolf Steiner Press 1973

By Sergei O. Prokofieff:

May Human Beings Hear It!, *The Mystery of the Christmas Conference*, Temple Lodge Publishing 2004